I0420685

WISE UP AMERICA!

How To Vote For The President Of The United States

BY
NINA MARTIN

ISBN-13: 978-1518682513
ISBN-10: 1518682510

Cover and interior design by: Shina Chen
First Edition 2015
Printed in the United States of America

TABLE OF CONTENTS

★ ★ ★

President of the United States.
Leader of the free world.
Arguably, the most important
job on the planet.
You will decide who it will be.

★ ★ ★

Are you ready?
Do you know HOW to vote for the next
President of the United States?

EVERY FOUR YEARS

★ ★ ★

Nearly eight years ago, a war-weary America decided it wanted change and voted in a man who promised it. He delivered. His sweeping overhaul of the country, however, left many citizens bewildered. Was this the change America had asked for? Or, did we unwittingly throw the baby out with the bathwater?

That candidate who rang the bell for change became our President. His second term is coming to a close, which presents us with a tantalizing opportunity – to once again cast our vote for the most important public post in the world.

Every four years, American citizens get a chance to be heard. By voting for the next President of the United States, we participate in an amazing privilege that comes with powerful consequences. This individual will be in control of our country and our lives for four straight years. Therefore, we cannot go into the voting booth lightly.

It's critical that we get to know the candidates well. These are the people who believe they should run our country and lead the free world. They want your vote. Who are you going to give it to?

The aim of this book is to help you answer this vital question. Once you've cast your vote, you've officially given that candidate your blessing to make decisions on your behalf. With your life and future in their hands, doesn't it make sense to get to know them?

For their part, they want to get to know you. Candidates travel all over the country to meet Americans face to face. They invest in television ads, participate in presidential debates and create websites that tell you exactly what they stand for. They disseminate information that tells you who they are, what they believe and how to think about them. Are you going to take it at face value? Remember, we're talking politics. Now ask yourself the question again. Are you going to swallow what they feed you, or are you going to check it out?

THE EASIEST JOB TO APPLY FOR. THE HARDEST TO HOLD.

★ ★ ★

Did you know that the qualifications to become President of the United States boils down to just three things[1]? He or she must be:

1)   A natural born citizen of the United States
2)   A resident for 14 years
3)   35 years of age or older

That's it. No college degree necessary. No military service required. No prerequisite of holding public office. Unlike any other job post in America, the position of U.S. President is completely open to interpretation regarding his or her education, real world experience, skill sets, and personality traits to successfully handle the post. Our President could just as easily be a former war hero, business tycoon, peanut farmer or even a movie star.

Since there are no pre-qualifications that define the job, it falls to American citizens to make that determination. That's you. You're the boss. You have a part in hiring the person who will be calling the shots for America.

Since the President is responsible for the welfare of more than approximately 320 million people[2] including you, what do you think his or her qualifications should be? This isn't the time to fall back on your intuition, someone else's opinion or presidential good looks. Whoever sits in the Oval Office has the power to pass new laws, increase taxes, start a war and then send you to fight it. And that's just the tip of the iceberg. In the wrong hands, that power can be catastrophic with fallout felt for decades and even generations.

Make sure the right person represents you and your loved ones in Washington D.C.

Make time to do a Background Check.

[1]Library of Congress http://www.loc.gov/teachers/classroommaterials/presentationsandactivities/presentations/elections/candid.html

[2]United States Census Bureau http://www.census.gov/popclock

THE BACKGROUND CHECK

★ ★ ★

When the Human Resources department for a corporation considers hiring someone for a job, they perform a background check first. They verify former employment. Call references. Surf the Internet to assess the "lifestyle" of this new hire. They want to know if this person is the right fit and that nothing in his or her past could expose the company or its employees to risk. The same should be done with presidential candidates.

Now, you're probably thinking this is the job of the news media. They should be doing the legwork for us, right? Unfortunately, today's media is more inclined to share "infotainment" with you than unbiased investigative reporting or hard news. Providing celebrity opinions and one-sided viewpoints gets more attention, more ratings and more advertising revenue. To ensure you have a solid foundation upon which to base your own opinion of presidential candidates, you should do a little homework of your own. Here's **HOW**.

Google them. Run a search on Bing, Yahoo!™ or any web search engine. It's fast. It's fun. It can be very revealing. Dozens of websites and links to articles will come up. What should you ask? Here are some sample search queries:

1. Is (candidate) married? Divorced? Children?

2. Does (candidate) have military experience?

3. What is his/her education?

4. Has (candidate) ever been arrested?

5. Is (candidate) an activist? If so, what is their cause?

6. Does (candidate) support charities or philanthropies?

7. Is (candidate) involved in community service?

8. Has (candidate) ever used drugs?

9. What are some of his/her biggest achievements?

10. What are some of his/her biggest mistakes?

Visit social media sites. Facebook, Pinterest, Instagram, Flickr, Google+, LinkedIn®, and other social media networks are places to get a pulse on candidates. What is the candidate saying about himself or herself? What are people saying about them? If you search "Hillary Clinton" on Pinterest, you'll find everything from accolades and scandals to vintage videos and Hillary refrigerator magnets.

Social media is not vetted for accuracy, so it's important to resist the temptation to rest your opinion on any one post. Think like a true journalist and try to find two sides to every story. Only then can you adequately begin the process of formulating your own opinion.

Explore politicians' track records. Politicians talk a lot. The trick is finding out if their words match up to their actions. Find out. The websites listed here make it easy and put some juicy information right at your fingertips. You can see:

- Who shows up to work and who doesn't
- How they vote
- What bills or resolutions they have sponsored
- Committees they sit on

You'll discover a great deal in a matter of minutes. For real time information on candidates who currently hold an office in Congress, check out any of these resources:

Vote Smart – Just The Facts
https://votesmart.org

Find voting records, bios, issue positions, interest group ratings, public statements and campaign finances.

Track the Unites States Congress
https://www.govtrack.us

See what bills have failed, passed a vote, and/or been enacted. GovTrack forecasts a bill's chance of getting enacted and also provides contact information to call or email the legislators about the bill.

THOMAS
http://thomas.loc.gov/home/abt_thom.html

A veritable mountain of information on everything from Bills and Resolutions to Public Laws, House and Senate Roll Call Votes, and more.

OPEN CONGRESS
https://www.opencongress.org

Track legislation as well as interact with other interested parties if you wish to be involved in the process.

Watch televised debates. This is the perfect opportunity to hear how candidates respond to questions that are important to Americans such as: how to improve the economy, create jobs, manage tensions in the Middle East, protect the planet from global warming and much more. Examine not just what they say but how they handle the questions. Are they polite and considerate? Conversational or confrontational? Clear and concise? Obscure and long-winded? Do they talk to you in politician-speak ("narrative that resonates with the populace") or plain English ("ideas that connect with the people")? During a debate, listen and watch closely to the candidates then ask yourself: Could they handle the job? Could they run my country successfully?

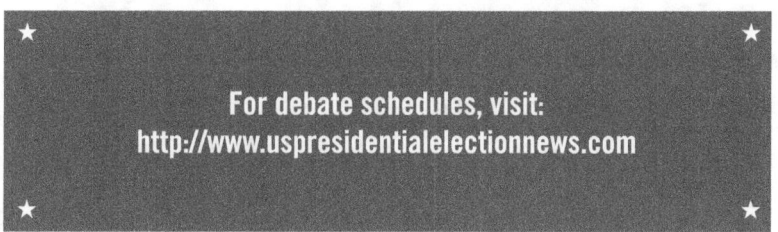

For debate schedules, visit:
http://www.uspresidentialelectionnews.com

Information is only as good as the source. Make sure you trust the source that delivers the content you're searching. Some search queries will deliver straight up, factual answers. Others will be subjective. For instance, if you search: "What are some of Ben Carson's biggest accomplishments?" you'll get a whole host of answers because the question is interpretive. Here is what a Google search turned up:

www.physicianspractice.com -- Ben Carson a Story of Accomplishment Against All Odds…important to be persistent and to know which risks are the best ones to take.."

www.biography.com/people/ben-carson -- Ben Carson has journeyed from troubled youth to gifted neurosurgeon, known for his work separating conjoined twins.

www.hopkinschildrens.org -- Received Medal of Freedom…and co-founder of the Carson Scholars Fund, which recognizes young people of all backgrounds for exceptional academic and humanitarian accomplishments…His three books, Gifted Hands, Think BIG and The Big Picture offer inspiration…

www.icr.org -- Benjamin S. Carson, M.D. one of the world's foremost pediatric neurosurgeons, Dr. Carson was also selected by CNN and Time as one of the nation's top 20…

It's clear from this search that a variety of media outlets place a different emphasis on what they deem are Ben Carson's biggest achievements—from his persistence in overcoming nearly insurmountable odds to becoming a renowned surgeon, author and philanthropist. This is a positive example, but what happens when you explore more challenging territory? For example: "What are some of Marco Rubio's biggest mistakes?" Google delivered the following:

www.thenewamerican.com -- Marco Rubio's big immigration mistake...

www.westernjournalism.com -- Going from being a Tea Party hero to an apologist for the gang of eight...

www.bloomberg.com -- The very issue thought would be a game-changing, legacy builder looks like a big liability...

www.msnbc.com -- Jeb vs. Marco

www.washingtonpost.com -- At issue is whether Rubio flip-flopped in his views on Iraq...

Obviously, the media places a different emphasis on what they see as Marco Rubio's biggest mistakes. Try to be impartial as you sift through information. Be open to viewpoints. What you'll come to discover in doing your own research on candidates is that you have opinions on the issues. You will find candidates who stand with you, and those against. It's a fascinating process and one that will ultimately reveal the right presidential candidate choice for you.

WOULD YOU REALLY VOTE
FOR THIS PERSON?

★ ★ ★

When people make decisions, they filter them through a set of qualifications. Take buying a car for example. You might weigh your decision on things like its safety record, gas consumption and whether or not it's made in America. Your neighbor, on the other hand, might want a sporty European import that turns heads and goes from 0 to 60 in five seconds flat.

Voting for the President is a similar exercise. Each of us evaluates candidates through our own set of criteria. To do that effectively, you need to know what that criterion is. You need to establish your own set of Presidential qualifications.

To begin that process, ask yourself some basic questions. What kind of individual would you like to see in the Oval Office? Is it someone who has the right balance of diplomacy and steely reserve to manage world affairs? Is it the equivalent of a Congress "whisperer" who can reach across the aisle and turn quarrelsome politicians back into civil servants?

There are no hard and fast rules for what makes a good President. Every four years, American citizens have to decide which qualifications are most important at that point in time. If the world is teetering on the edge of war, American citizens might do well to consider electing a President who understands the military, how it works and how to best utilize it to protect our interests at home and abroad. If our country is facing an economic collapse, maybe we need a President who has run a business, fixed broken companies and brought them back to life.

Each time Americans go to the polls to vote for their next President, our country is in a different place than it was four years prior. This is an important consideration when weighing in on the qualifications of the candidates. Based on where our country is today, what qualifications would be most beneficial for the next four years? **HOW** are you going to qualify candidates?

Break it down. With any large task, it's easier to get your arms around it when you break it down into smaller parts or steps. In this case, it's the qualifications that help you come to a decision about candidates. Build a list. It can be as long or as short as you deem necessary. This is YOUR list of criteria to help determine the best candidate for President of the United States. To get the wheels turning, here are a few qualifications to ponder:

1. **INTEGRITY** – Someone who lives by a moral compass.

2. **WISDOM** – Life experiences that provide foundational knowledge for decision-making.

3. **CONFIDENCE** – Able to respond calmly and decisively under pressure.

4. **ENDURANCE** – Has the energy and focus to manage 10-15 hour workdays.

5. **LEADERSHIP** - Ability to work with Congress and world leaders to advance America's vision.

These are examples of qualifications. You can keep them, replace them or add to them. But make a set of your own. You're going to need your qualifications for the last part of your presidential voting preparation:

The Filter Test.

THE FILTER TEST

★ ★ ★

Once you have established your list of qualifications, run your candidates through the Filter Test. In other words, a hypothetical crisis. Why a crisis? Anyone can manage the good times. It's the bad times that test us. They demonstrate our strengths and our weaknesses. Reveal our true worth.

Which of your candidates could make the hard decisions? Which one would have the backbone, intelligence and cooperation of Congress to handle crisis conditions? In worse case hypothetical scenarios, you are the judge and jury. You'll have to rely on your research and qualifications list to speculate who could rise to the occasion and who could potentially fail. A Filter Test puts your candidate in the Situation Room. So, **HOW** do you perform a Filter Test?

1 Select your top candidates

2 Create hypothetical scenarios for them to manage

3 Filter the scenarios through your set of qualifications and your research

---

Filter Test Example

1) Let's say you're considering Ted Cruz and Bernie Sanders

2) Your hypothetical scenarios are as follows:
   - Terrorists just bombed a major U.S. port
   - Congress is threatening a government shutdown
   - The Eastern seaboard is hit by a Category 5 hurricane
   - Iran refuses inspections of its nuclear facilities

3) Filter your candidates through each scenario based on your list of qualifications and the research you've done

---

Look at your answers. How do you think Ted Cruz would handle a terrorist attack or a government shutdown? Bernie Sanders a natural disaster or a nuclear threat? Would one candidate consistently rise to the occasion? You may have your answer for U.S President. Is it split down the middle? Consider your candidate's party.

PARTY TIME

★ ★ ★

The United States government is currently ruled by two political parties—Republican and Democrat. Yes, we have other parties like Libertarian, Green, Constitution and even the Tea Party. Have these other parties ever won the Presidency? Not yet. In the current political climate, pragmatism rules that you should cast your ballot for the Democrat or the Republican nominee if you want your vote to count. If neither party aligns with your beliefs or principles, you can vote for a candidate from another party. The question to ask yourself is this: Do you give your vote to someone who has little hope of winning the day, or is it better to vote for the lesser of two evils? Only you can decide.

This book does not advocate joining a political party one way or the other. However, it is important to understand the core beliefs of the ruling political parties in order to know **HOW** to vote for the President of the United States.

THE REPUBLICAN PARTY

The Republican Party started in the 1850s and is often referred to as the **G**rand **O**ld **P**arty (GOP). It stands for limited government. It's about free enterprise, free markets and individual rights—encouraging independent initiative to achieve prosperity and success. This translates to a strong focus on government at the state and community level and a light touch at the Federal level. It is considered a Conservative party and stands for:

- Traditional definitions of marriage between a man and a woman
- Pro-Life regarding abortion
- The right to keep and bear arms (guaranteed under the Constitution)
- Less taxation
- Simpler tax code favoring a flat tax
- Conservation efforts that balance with the economy
- Increased military spending

Interesting Republican Trivia:

- Abraham Lincoln was the first Republican President in 1860*
- It was the first political party to favor women's suffrage*

* Republican Views on The Issues
  http://www.republicanviews.org/what-is-a-republican-republican-definition

THE DEMOCRATIC PARTY

The Democratic Party, created in 1848, believes strength is in numbers – when people combine their efforts for the greater good of the community. If any word captures the spirit of Democrats it is "fair"—getting your fair share and playing by the same rules. This translates to big government—creating programs at the national level and minimizing the power of state and local government. In the past, it was considered the liberal party, but in recent years the term most often used is "progressive" and the party supports:

- Same-sex marriage as well as traditional marriage
- Pro-Choice regarding abortion
- Stricter gun control laws
- Taxation to fund federal programs
- Progressive taxation relative to the income bracket
- Climate change legislation
- Decreased military spending

Interesting Democrat Trivia:

- In 1920 under the presidency of Democrat, Woodrow Wilson, women got the right to vote
- Democrat President Franklin D. Roosevelt was the architect of the New Deal after the Great Depression

* Democrats https://www.democrats.org/about/our-party
www.diffen.com/difference/Democrat_vs_Republican

In the summer of 2016, the ruling political parties will have their national conventions to nominate their Presidential candidate. Prior to the conventions, state primaries and caucuses deliver clues as to whom the public thinks should rise to the top. At the conventions, delegates can vote for only one nominee, and it is usually representative of their state's leaning. Things can and do get exciting when the race is close and multiple rounds of balloting take place. Following are the upcoming 2016 conventions:

Republican Convention
July 18-21 in Cleveland, OH*

★ ★ ★

Democrat Convention
Week of July 25 in Philadelphia, PA*

The interesting thing about the political party system in America is how consistent it actually is. History demonstrates that when America leans too much to the left (DEM) or too much to the right (REP), it swings the other way to counter-balance extremism. In other words, America self-corrects to ensure the principles upon which the nation was founded are preserved.

* http://2016.presidential-election.info/conventions/

WHEN TO START PREPPING

★ ★ ★

How long does it take to prepare to vote? There is no right or wrong amount of time. Take a year, a month or a week. The point is to feel confident and self-assured when you mail in your absentee ballot or walk into the voting booth.

You can start your candidate education during the primaries, or you can wait until the national conventions make their nominee choice. There is no wrong time to get informed. If you want to ease into it, give yourself several months so you can pace yourself. This allows you to use downtime proactively to check out what the candidates are saying and doing (think daily commute, lunch hour, in-between classes, late night insomnia, etc.). With today's mobile digital devices like tablets, laptops and smartphones, you can get information on the go. Visit social media sites. Watch the debates. Tune into different media outlets like Fox News, CNN and MSNBC. Talk with friends, family and professional colleagues to get outside perspective.

If you're a procrastinator, you can still arm yourself with knowledge in the weeks leading up to Election Day. The point is to pull the voting lever knowing you are making the best decision to support you and your family. You want to be ready to vote for the 45th U.S. President on November 8th, 2016.

This book gives you the **HOW**. Now it's up to you to take control of your power and do what others all over the globe wish they could do:

Vote for the President of the United States of America.

PREP MATERIALS

★ ★ ★

The Background Check

Qualifications

The Filter Test

CANDIDATE 1

1. Is (candidate) married? Divorced? Children?

2. Does (candidate) have military experience?

3. What is his/her education?

4. Has (candidate) ever been arrested?

5. Is (candidate) an activist? If so, what is their cause?

6. Does (candidate) support charities or philanthropies?

7. Is (candidate) involved in community service?

8. Has (candidate) ever used drugs?

9. What are some of his/her biggest achievements?

10. What are some of his/her biggest mistakes?

CANDIDATE 2

1. Is (candidate) married? Divorced? Children?

2. Does (candidate) have military experience?

3. What is his/her education?

4. Has (candidate) ever been arrested?

5. Is (candidate) an activist? If so, what is their cause?

6. Does (candidate) support charities or philanthropies?

7. Is (candidate) involved in community service?

8. Has (candidate) ever used drugs?

9. What are some of his/her biggest achievements?

10. What are some of his/her biggest mistakes?

CANDIDATE 3

1. Is (candidate) married? Divorced? Children?

2. Does (candidate) have military experience?

3. What is his/her education?

4. Has (candidate) ever been arrested?

5. Is (candidate) an activist? If so, what is their cause?

6. Does (candidate) support charities or philanthropies?

7. Is (candidate) involved in community service?

8. Has (candidate) ever used drugs?

9. What are some of his/her biggest achievements?

10. What are some of his/her biggest mistakes?

CANDIDATE 4

1. Is (candidate) married? Divorced? Children?

2. Does (candidate) have military experience?

3. What is his/her education?

4. Has (candidate) ever been arrested?

5. Is (candidate) an activist? If so, what is their cause?

6. Does (candidate) support charities or philanthropies?

7. Is (candidate) involved in community service?

8. Has (candidate) ever used drugs?

9. What are some of his/her biggest achievements?

10. What are some of his/her biggest mistakes?

BACKGROUND CHECK WORKSHEET 2

ISSUES	CANDIDATE 1
Foreign Policy	
Job Creation	
Defense/Military	
Social Security/ Entitlements	
Immigration	
Homeland Security/ Terrorism	
Healthcare	
Tax Reform	
Marijuana Legalization	
Gay Rights	
Abortion	

BACKGROUND CHECK WORKSHEET 2

ISSUES	CANDIDATE 2
Foreign Policy	
Job Creation	
Defense/Military	
Social Security/ Entitlements	
Immigration	
Homeland Security/ Terrorism	
Healthcare	
Tax Reform	
Marijuana Legalization	
Gay Rights	
Abortion	

BACKGROUND CHECK WORKSHEET 2

ISSUES	CANDIDATE 3
Foreign Policy	
Job Creation	
Defense/Military	
Social Security/Entitlements	
Immigration	
Homeland Security/Terrorism	
Healthcare	
Tax Reform	
Marijuana Legalization	
Gay Rights	
Abortion	

BACKGROUND CHECK WORKSHEET 2

ISSUES	CANDIDATE 4
Foreign Policy	
Job Creation	
Defense/Military	
Social Security/ Entitlements	
Immigration	
Homeland Security/ Terrorism	
Healthcare	
Tax Reform	
Marijuana Legalization	
Gay Rights	
Abortion	

THE FILTER TEST

CANDIDATE 1

Question 1:

Answer:

Success_____ Failure_____

Question 2:

Answer:

Success_____ Failure_____

Question 3:

Answer:

Success_____ Failure_____

Question 4:

Answer:

Success_____ Failure_____

Question 5:

Answer:

Success_____ Failure_____

Tally up candidate successes and failures.

CANDIDATE 1
Success _____
Failure _____

Did one candidate rise above the other? If so, you may want to give serious consideration to that candidate.

38

CANDIDATE 2

Question 1:

Answer:

Success_____ Failure_____

Question 2:

Answer:

Success_____ Failure_____

Question 3:

Answer:

Success_____ Failure_____

Question 4:

Answer:

Success_____ Failure_____

Question 5:

Answer:

Success_____ Failure_____

Tally up candidate successes and failures.

CANDIDATE 2

Success _____

Failure _____

Did one candidate rise above the other? If so, you may want to give serious consideration to that candidate.

CANDIDATE 3

Question 1:

Answer:

Success_____ Failure_____

Question 2:

Answer:

Success_____ Failure_____

Question 3:

Answer:

Success_____ Failure_____

Question 4:

Answer:

Success_____ Failure_____

Question 5:

Answer:

Success_____ Failure_____

Tally up candidate successes and failures.

CANDIDATE 3
Success _____
Failure _____

Did one candidate rise above the other? If so, you may want to give serious consideration to that candidate.

THE FILTER TEST

CANDIDATE 4

Question 1:

Answer:

Success_____ Failure_____

Question 2:

Answer:

Success_____ Failure_____

Question 3:

Answer:

Success_____ Failure_____

Question 4:

Answer:

Success_____ Failure_____

Question 5:

Answer:

Success_____ Failure_____

Tally up candidate successes and failures.

CANDIDATE 4
Success _____
Failure _____

Did one candidate rise above the other? If so, you may want to give serious consideration to that candidate.

ABOUT THE AUTHOR

Nina Martin is a 30-year veteran of the advertising industry and founder of MNM Studios, a marketing and design firm in Southern California. This is her first published book, one she felt compelled to write in light of the forthcoming presidential election. She lives in Orange County with her husband, daughter and family Cavachon.

www.ingramcontent.com/pod-product-compliance
Lightning Source LLC
Chambersburg PA
CBHW061801280526
45787CB00003BA/1439